EATING PALEO, KETO, AND VEGAN

Cookbook

Jefery Ramon

PAGE PUBLISHING
Conneaut Lake, PA

First originally published by Page Publishing 2022

ISBN 979-8-88654-010-9 (pbk)
ISBN 979-8-88793-698-7 (hc)
ISBN 979-8-88654-014-7 (digital)

Printed in the United States of America

Contents

Thanks and Special Thanks

My thanks and special thanks to those who gave me the understanding of being the best of myself. As I was the vegan and organic chef in a New York City restaurant, it gave me some of the knowledge I needed to further my understanding for a better and healthier living and share with those people and loyal customers who care about their well-being. My special thanks to my friend in Thessaloniki, Greece, who is one of the Pateras family. She was magnificent, and she showed me the real meaning of eating vegan food and shared with those who didn't know the real meaning of eating fresh and unprocessed foods. I traveled in Greece, learning about the real homemade and the original and real organic fresh seafood and vegetables that were one of the best ways to be introduced to the real Mediterranean cookeries. The passion I have for organic and vegan foods and then to be able to share with others is unlimited. Then to know the acceptance from the public or to many who are just learning of its benefits, it is also more clear that it has its benefits, and others are being more appreciative of its good being. Thanks to those who came in every day just to have my vegan and organic creation and who helped me know that whatever I was doing, it was the right thing to have lots of varieties and the combinations and choices that were at their disposal. I also would like to thank all those who have helped me with my food endeavor, and to those, I wish to pay my respects.

Acknowledgments

I would like to acknowledge the beautiful people who walked me through each step when I didn't know the way, meaning to be the best chef and to be good at what I was doing.

CEO Joe at Kettlebellkitchen, who was there in most ways; CEO Yela at Organique, who has seen in me what I didn't see or know; and also Chef Chastitanuo from Thessaloniki, Greece, who gave me the right of way to learn more about having the best ingredients on the plate and the real Mediterranean food and to show me that fresh fish or seafood is best when out of the water. Living and traveling back and forth to Greece was spectacular, something that cannot be forgotten, and every time I get the chance, even if I only stay for a few days, it's wonderful.

My special acknowledgment also goes out to my good friend Abdullah, whose mom is also vegan in Jordan and who gave me the best tours I've ever had of Petra and the other old cities I was able to see along the river of Jordan, where it is said Jesus was baptized. I would also like to give thanks to Azmaniel, a friend from Morocco who helped to show me the vegan diet when I had a very bad case of acne. After that diet, it helped me get rid of acne—something doctors worked on with me and never helped, but that vegan diet helped, and now twenty years later, it hasn't returned.

About Knowing

In the past, I've spoken to a few people who thought they were paleo just because they were eating less meats or no meat at all and only were eating fish, but then I had to tell them that was not paleo. With paleo, you are allowed to eat as much meat as you want, but it would come down to eating dairy products. Paleo or being vegan is not as easy as you would think because, as I wrote before and have stressed in my *Hosting the Holidays* cookbook, those diets are and must be respected not only because of choices but also of what people believe in and because it's a diet that is good for you.

As you may notice in my book, I'm not a person who gives too much complicated explanations in preparing something. This is something an Austrian chef showed me back in Europe. He said you must get to the point because some people would get bored quickly.

Introduction—to the New Food

Up until 2018, I've spoken to many people, and some don't know what are vegan or paleo foods or the difference between vegan and paleo, and for that reason, I am calling this section "Introduction—to the New Foods."

As a food enthusiast or aficionado who loves the essentials, the infatuation, and the thrills of new up-and-coming dining and cooking ideas, I was very happy to be the chef of one of the leading distributers of paleo foods in the northeast. From vegan and organic to healthy foods then to paleo foods, I was very happy to share with those people who took part in loving every meal they consumed from the creations that were sent to them on a weekly basis. The energy and the thought behind making the best that money can buy and the best that could come out of a kitchen and the best that we can put in our bodies, foods that was made with love and determination to make it the best to all the consumers we served and to have served them all as VIP at all times. The healthy choices and the best knowledge of the paleo idea that was given, you will find like no others in this book. You will find recipes like nobody else recipes. They are recipes that focus on you, on making you healthier and for you to keep on the right track and make the right choice when grocery shopping or ordering in.

To be able to introduce new foods, we must be able to introduce the combinations of new foods, food without food colorings, foods without hormones, foods without dairies, and foods that cater to a better, healthier living. One of the best ways to healthier living is to know how to balance the portions we eat and know the healthy fats found in nuts, eggs, some oils, and seeds. Our better choice in lean meats, fish, and the way we cook them is also a factor in the way we should use, and to stay away from pasta and pasta products is also another way for us to look at the way we choose to add any carbs to our bodies and our way of life.

New food means a new beginning, a new way of making the right choice and a new you. Let me take you on the journey of better foods, better choices, and better ways of thinking about what to eat and how much to eat. We may all eat up to five meals a day but with a balanced diet and a measured amount in the course of our day.

What Is Vegan?

Vegan is not just another way of eating but is another way of choosing vegan foods that do not associate themselves with any kind of meats.

A person who is vegan does not see it as a diet but as a way of life and the choicest they have made—no dairy products, no animal products or kinds of wheat.

Vegan, like organic or paleo or even a vegetarian, has a much shorter food choice because of the strict restrictions they may have in their way of food choices.

Veganism is said to be a kind of diet, but in the eyes of a vegan person, it's not a diet but a way of life and is known not to associate itself with the commodity in animal status and to reject the philosophy of the practice that can be obtained from animals.

They do not associate themselves with any kind of animal product. In addition, the bottom line is not to associate themselves; their dietary is not to consume meats. Vegan is not thought to be an obligation but a choice that many people make, but it's also known to be subscribed after some people develop allergies to animal by-products or dairy.

Vegan is…

Vegan is not only a way of life but the choices and needs people make. You may have people that are vegan by choice and beliefs and others by need in their own diets, and I respect that even if some of us do enjoy a scrambled or boiled egg for breakfast.

Vegan is not for everyone. Even people eat meat in the past and after a few years or after trying to go vegan and have stayed vegan.

What Is Gluten?

Gluten is a substance found in some cereals and cereal grains and causes illness in people with celiac disease. Gluten is also a group of proteins found in cereals grains that occur in wheat species such as spelt, Khorasan, emmer, einkorn, triticale, barley, rye, and oats.

Gluten is a big no when it comes to a person with celiac disease. A person with that kind of illness should not even have gluten on their place as we all know gluten is a general name for proteins found in wheat (wheatberries), durum, emmer, semolina, spelt, farro, rye, and others. You may also look up online. You may also go to your library or online, in your Wikipedia.

These groups of proteins are called prolamins and glutelins and are compromised by 75–85 percent of the total protein found in bread. The gluten found in rice can maize but can differ from true gluten. There are many people who suffer from gluten. Gluten can trigger adverse inflammatory immunological and autoimmune reactions in some people and is related to disorders such as celiac disease and non-celiac gluten sensitivity. These disorders are treated by gluten-free diets.

What Is or Why Paleo?

Why paleo? Because it's a better way of keeping track of your healthier you. Paleo is also a lifestyle and is another approach to diet without compromising the food you may like best.

Unlike vegan diets, it does exclude foods from agriculture but mimics the foods of our ancestors. We mostly naturally like foods that are not good for our bodies. It's like a natural instinct but is also something we have modernized and that has evolved in the past decade.

Paleo is also like a benefited genetic improved habit we all naturally have and allows us to enjoy the moderated healthy fats, along with nuts, seeds, lots of protein, and not to miss the artificial sweeteners and the sugary drinks and additives.

With paleo, we can't have anything that has sugar, molasses, honey, or agave, even just a small amount. Keeping healthy and fit is the goal of a paleo diet, along with exercise and lots of water. As a former paleo chef in NYC, the ultimate goal of all customers was to keep fit and to stick to their respective streaked diets that, at times, were fascinating to witness and to be a part of.

Also, in paleo and eating, you want to stay focused on having in your meals non-starchy carbs, stay heart-healthy, and keep the general rule in mind of protein and low or non-starchy foods.

Paleo is a very good diet. In a way, some people cannot afford paleo because it has its restrictions and its limits, restrictions in what to eat and limited choices. Limiting doesn't mean for a few but what can be eaten, for example, dairy products and starches.

Every moment I've had cooking, sharing and showing others was my great pleasure, and if I have it all to do again, I will be more than happy to do it.

The Information List on a Healthier You

A superfood for the brain

Cold water fish like salmon	
Avocado	Exotic berries
Egg yolks	Walnuts
Chlorella	Grass-fed beef
Hemp seeds	Coconut oil

Normal day-to-day foods with lots of iron

Beets	Parsley	Brussels sprouts	Tomatoes
Almonds	Bananas	Avocado	Hemp Seeds
Kale	Grapes	Apricots	Collard greens
Bok choy	Broccoli	Figs	Sprouts
Pine Nuts	Pumpkin Seeds	Green Beans	Swiss chard
Chia Seeds	Potatoes	Spinach	Sunflower Seeds

Healthier juices and/or smoothies and the benefits they can impose

Sicknesses	Remedy that helps
Arthritis	eat lots of carrots, pineapples, lemon, and celery
Ulcer helper	celery, cabbage, and carrots
Stress helper	bananas, pear, and strawberries

Nervousness	pomegranate, celery, and carrots
Asthma relief	lots of garlic, carrots, apples, and spinach
Fatigue	lemons, spinach, beets, carrots, and green apples
Depression	spinach, carrots, apples, and beets
Indigestion	carrots, pineapple, mint, and lemon

The General Rule in Knife Handling

Cut and slice with care, hold the knife correctly, hold the handle with three fingers, and have your index finger and thumb on opposite sides of the blade. Stand with your body over the table and your eyes on the product. Keep the knife touching the cutting board and gradually move the knife sideways across the product on the cutting board. Use the tip of the knife for delicate work and small items. This may not feel correct at first, but after several cuts of using mostly the tips and heel of the knife on the product you're cutting, that weird feeling will then come to pass.

In switching from one task to another, keep in mind not to have cross contamination because when working with food, it's easy to spread germs that can easily make you sick. Washing your hands and cleaning your cutting board, along with sanitizing your knives, are good things for you and your guest or your customers. These are what we should all be doing.

Chef's knife, paring knife, and slicer are all in many ways different when handling. They do not come as stacking as when we would use a butcher knife or a clever but not to confuse when using to avoid cutting your finger or hand. Precision cutting is always the key in using a knife not to overwhelm ourselves and not to be anxious and then cut ourselves. At first, we must all take our time. Then when the time is right, we should take action. In neither of my books I will ever use too many terms because I don't believe in terms because after all the countries I've been to and worked, we all use our knives in the way we want, just too many of us forget the country we live in and the way we all develop in ourselves when cooking slicing and mixing.

What We Shouldn't Eat as Vegan People

As a vegan person, no kind of meat should or could be consumed, including fish, poultry, game birds, eggs of no kind, or dairy products.

Vegan is a streaked diet and must at all times be kept, not only because of vegan but also because there may be reasons a person is vegan. It could be allergies or doctors' orders. We may never know. And for that reason, if a person says he or she is a vegan, we must change cutting boards, knives, and in some cases plates and not cook or fry in the same pot or frying pan where we had cooked animal by-products.

- Absolutely no animal products
- No meats, no dairy, no eggs, no cheeses
- No peanut butter, no soy product
- No whey protein (not all fruits are good) and less of those that are full of glycemic loads, and you must always try to avoid genetically modified organism fruits

After speaking to a few veganism in the past, some have told me they ate coconuts, and others said they didn't, which was not clear to me if they did or did not, but to my understanding, they did because it has nothing to do with animal by-product, and I don't know anybody who has allergies from coconut. I do know a few people with allergies to pineapples, and the most common is nuts.

What We Shouldn't Eat
as Paleo People

As paleo people, we can't eat soybean oil, artificial sweeteners, processed meats, kinds of butter, whole kinds of wheat, grains, cheeses, deli meats, whey proteins (unless grass-fed whey), barley, millets, oatmeals, lentils, no kind of cereals, hummus unless made from vegetables, no kinds of beans, chickpeas, manias, black-eyed peas, tapioca, high-fructose corn syrup, soft drinks, quinoa, snow peas, corn amaranth, buckwheat cassava root, potatoes, dried fruit, and all processed foods with dairy and protein. These are not all what we as paleo people shouldn't eat but does cover most of the non-eating ingredients we have from our paleo diet. In some cases, quinoa, snow, or snap peas are accepted.

All Processed Foods

No dairy such as cheese, butter milk, soy product, yogurt, ice cream, sorghum, buckwheat, snow peas, manioc, dried fruit, lentils, millet, rye, legumes, grains, agave nectar, and stevia—these may not be all what a conscious person should avoid, but it's a map of the most avoidable products.

The Keto Diet—Is It a Lifestyle, or Is It a Diet or a Way of Life?

The keto diet is known to many as the ketogenic diet, of which I disagree with for many reasons but is in many ways a diet to many. Respectfully, the keto diet has similarities to paleo nutrition's value and a lot of the paleo characteristics. And as a former paleo and organic chef, I take that very seriously and the way I make myself submit to nutrition and cookery.

We can learn a lot if we explore more foods and the way they are prepared and also the way we digest what we eat. I find too many food explorers, writers, and chefs don't think about the digestive system of others and the way they digest their foods. Because we are humans, our systems are not all the same, and we have our own way of digesting foods. I find the celiac and its gluten-free diet does come in handy because of the no seasoning or just a few seasonings and no gluten, which is great nutrition and a well-balanced diet when done the right way.

In my professional opinion, I think the keto diet is a natural way of losing weight in a long time period. I've recommended to friends in the past the paleo diet and the keto diet advantage that would help them who were struggling with weight loss, and it helped them not only lose weight but also keep it off and make better choices when shopping. As we know, the keto diet is a naturally occurring ingredient some that like the keto diet salt something that forces the body into a constant state of ketosis. The low of natural process is a process of the body that initiates foods to survive the ketosis that constantly burns carbs and fat in the liver. There is so much that is good for us in the keto diet foods and a lot that we don't know yet but use what we know, and because a lot of us live in big cities, we only use what is to our disposal.

Is Celiac a Disease or a Genetic Disorder?

In my oath to writing and trying to solve some of the eating issues, I've seen many people with food and their allergies. In the year 2015, as I was the head chef at Kettlebellkitchen, we had an employee whose allergies were so bad that if she was to smell a pineapple, she would get frantic and begin to get swollen in the face. In the beginning, when I was first introduced to celiac vegan, I thought they were the same, but after I began to study and to learn more through research, it was clear to me that they were not the same. Steps can be taken to control celiac by adopting a gluten-free diet and, at times, not noticeable because they tend to get or become accustomed to passing loose stools and bowel movements.

A friend of mine from the Patera family in Greece was celiac with whom I had dined on many occasions back in the 1900s of which I didn't know at the time what it was, but a few months later, after the first time she told me about her allergies, I had a better understanding what it was. She is and was not the only person I got to know with those issues but also had the privilege to meet others like a friend from Split back from Croatia where freshness is taken very seriously.

You can find more information on celiac at www.BeyondCeliac.org for this diagnosis and treatment.

All celiac (recipient) people with celiac know they have an intolerance to gliadin, a gluten found in some grains like barley, some oats, and rye. Not being a doctor, I would advise you to be very careful because the body can be vulnerable to multiple sclerosis, osteoporosis, infertility, migraines, epilepsy, and type-1 diabetes. It involves

some intestines and the digestive process. I hope this was more help-
ful to all those celiac sufferers and would watch their respective diets
closely. After my research on celiac and its effects, I've learned more
to respect those people I have met along the way. Many may not
show or it may not be noticeable from the outside, but after conver-
sations with people who do have the disease, I feel for all of them and
understand what they feel and have a tremendous amount of respect
for them.

Best in Protein

As paleo people, we love our protein, lean meats, and premium cuts.

USDA and USDA organic is usually your best choice in buying your meats. I would also recommend buying your meats local, grass-fed, wild fish, game birds, free-roaming chickens, London broil, top sirloin, scallops, lobsters, shrimps, bison, lots of fish, including sweet or saltwater fish, eggs, or egg whites, buffalo meat, and venison. Grass-fed beef or pork is always the best for paleo lovers.

Lamb wild game organ meats bacon with no nitrates, gluten, or soy.

Specialty deli meats with no sugars, gluten or soy can be, at times, hard to find. Having your own neighborhood butcher is always the best. In that way, you know you will not be cheated for any cheaper or imitations meats like crabmeat.

Lean beef cuts, lean pork cuts like tenderloin and boneless chops, lean chicken, turkey breast, lean beef tenderloin no fat whatsoever, at times, are easy to find but could depend on where you are. The best is always, when possible, to have your butcher cut or slice to order your cuts of lean choice of meat. Wild game like pheasant and duck are all good, including farm-raised hen that is grass- or corn-fed. Even if corn is not in a Paleo diet, it's okay to eat hen or duck that has eaten corn. Hen is always somewhat sweet in flavor but very rich.

In my own daily food consumption, I've substituted meat for avocado and have had it instead of meat, which also makes it nice. I think avocado is a good side dish or a good substitute when there is no other protein around.

The (9) Shopping List

1. Paleo Short Shopping List

This list and the other list you will find in this book does not mean you should be limited to your paleo-eating practices.

Nuts and seeds
    Sunflower seeds
    Almonds
    Cashews
    Hazelnuts
    pumpkin seeds

Meats
    Chicken
    Beef
    Pork
    Goose
    Bear
    Deer
    Venison
    Wild boar
    Goat meat

Seafood
    Shrimps
    Tuna
    Salmon
    Oysters

Lobster
Mussels
Cod
Bass
Herring
Tilapia

Vegetables

Spinach
Lettuce
Mushrooms
Parsnips
Pumpkin
Sweet potatoes
Radishes
Squash
Tomatoes
Swish chard
Turnips
Mustard green
Broccoli
Celery
Collards
Brussels sprouts
Cabbage
Cauliflower
Fennel
Endive
Kale
Onions
Peppers
Rutabaga
Carrots
Artichokes
Bok choy
Beets
Asparagus
Fresh Herbs
Kohlrabi
Purslane
Chard
Garlic
Seaweed

Fruit

Apples
Avocado
Apricots
Banana
Calabash
Blackberries
Dates
Grapefruit
Grapes
Kiwi
Lemons
Limes
Papaya
Peaches
Orange
Pears
Pineapples
Plantain
Soursop (also known as guana-bana-graviola)
Star fruit
Cherries
Guava
Figs
Honeydew melon
Dates
Cherries
Acai
Mango
Blueberries
Pomegranate
Raspberries
Durian
Nectarine
Rhubarb
Strawberries

When choosing paleo, be sure to make the right choices like avoiding legumes, dairy, trans fats, caffeine, grains, salted meats and starches, and no refined sugars.

2. Low-Cholesterol Shopping List

This list is not intended to limit your shopping experience. It's only a guide for a better choice and experience when shopping.

Bread/Grains

Brown or wild rice, bagels, oatmeal, quinoa

Meats: Chicken breast, lean Pork meat

Tofu, canned tuna and all-white meat turkey virgin olive oil, tomatoes, salad dressings, peaches

Canned product: Artichokes, Beans, extra tomato paste, low sodium

Dairy: skim milk, low-fat cream, low-fat yogurt dark chocolate, nuts seeds onions, asparagus, oranges, pears, tomatoes, corn, potatoes, spinach, eggplant, melons pineapples potatoes, collards, garlic, greens

Snacks: popcorn, dried fruit, peanut butter, fresh fruits and veggies: bananas, apples, squash, herbs, broccoli, avocado, berries, cucumbers, asparagus mushrooms, lemons, Brussels sprouts

3. Sizes and Servings

Slice bread	1 slice	Pasta	1/2 c.
Rice	1/2 c.	Cereal	1/2 c.
Cooked Oatmeal	1/2 c.	Soup	1 c.
Gravy	2 tbsp.	Sauces	2 tbsp.
Mayonnaise	1 tbsp.	Coconut oil	1.5 tbsp.
Butter/Margarine	1 tbsp.	Egg/grade A	1 large

Cheese	2 slices	Milk	1 c.
Nuts	1/3 c.	Dark chocolate	2 oz.
Potato chips	1/4 c.	White meat chicken	6 oz.
Yogurt plain	1 c.	Peanut butter	2 tbsp.
Whitefish	6 oz.	Pink meat fish	2 tbsp.
Shellfish	1/2 lb.	Tofu	3 oz.
Cucumbers	6 oz.	Grapes	1/2 c.
Melons	1/2 c.	Avocado	1/2 c.
Sliced tomatoes	1/2 c.	Broccoli	1 c.
Pure fruit juice	1/2 c.	Artichokes	1/2 c.
Olives	12 tbsp.	Vegetable oil	6 tbsp.
Olive oil	6 tbsp.	Wine	1 c.
Black/green tea	1 c.	Coffee	1 c.
Berries	1/2 c.	Strawberries	1/2 c.

4.   Everyday Grocery List

Breakfast/Lunch

breads, bagel, oatmeal,
or cereals,
sausages, pancakes, yogurt
eggs, sour cream,
coconut milk
cauliflower, hummus, juices
apples, berries,
grapefruit, garlic
spinach, peas,
pears, broccoli

celery, peppers, carrots
cheese, nuts, seeds
mushrooms, soup
tea, ground port
peaches, oranges,
kiwi, sprouts
lettuce, tomatoes, bananas

Dinner

ground beef, chicken breast	salmon, tilapia, tuna,
vegetables, sweet potatoes	cod, sea bass
beets, Brussels sprouts,	yucca, snow peas,
	cauliflower
	carrots, celery, asparagus
	collards greens

5. What's Needed in the Pantry

gluten-free pasta, brown rice	nuts, oatmeal, arrowroot
cocoa, fresh garlic, lemons,	turmeric, curry powder,
unsweetened chocolate,	white peppercorns
dried parsley,	nutmeg powder,
kosher salt, extra virgin	ground cinnamon,
olive oil, almond milk,	marjoram, granulated
sweet paprika, light chicken	garlic, onion powder
broth, tomato paste,	beef broth, vanilla extract,
canned crushed tomatoes,	maple syrup, fresh ginger,
powder, peanut butter,	ginger powder, mustard
dried oregano, canned tuna	canned or condensed
	soups, mace pimentos

6. Pantry Substitutions List

arrowroot	instant tapioca or cornstarch
cup brown sugar	1/2 molasses
butter	vegetable oil
coconut oil	lard
corn syrup	honey
lemon juice	lime juice
1 lemon zest	1/2 tablespoon lemon extract
vanilla extract	50% maple syrup, 50% almond extract

7. Diabetic Short Shopping List

low-sodium crackers,
brown rice
poultry, lean ground
beef, soy milk
sugar-free pudding,
sugar- and salt-free
chicken broth
gluten-free pasta,
nuts, diet tea
fresh fruit, fresh vegetables

cereals, oatmeal, whole
wheat bread
eggs, low-fat milk,
sugar-free Jell-O
pineapple, canned juices,
no added sugar
dairy-free sugar-free ice cream,
lean pork, canned
tuna in water,
low salt canned
vegetables and quinoa

8. Shopping for Vegans

lentils, baba
ghanoush, bagels
egg substitute, Wasa crackers
soy cheese, soy
coffee creamer,
dried fruit, rice cakes,
orange juice

sweet potato pudding,
vegan seitan
marinated mushrooms,
vegan mayonnaise
vegan granola, soy
chip, dried veggies
cranberry juice, mocha,
vegan chicken patties

9. No Gluten Grocery List

quinoa, rice, flaxseeds,
corn margarine, rice cakes,
dried fruit free beer, eggs,
gluten-free pudding
corn chips, juice, red wine,
quinoa oils, arrowroot
powder, honey

strawberries, blueberries,
kiwi, butter or sunflower
seeds, popcorn, Jell-O,
gluten- gluten-free flour,
nut butter, cheese, syrup
beans, gluten-free soup,
canned milk, olive
shellfish, jam, buckwheat,
gluten-free waffle

How to Safely Hand a Knife to Somebody

Knives come in many shapes and different sizes. We should make it a habit to safely hand knives to others.

When handing a knife to somebody, have the knife pointing downward and then to the station table, then allow the other person to take the knife. We should not practice handing a knife to another person from hand to hand.

If and when storing your knife, make sure to store the knife in a knife storing only, and if you are in a professional kitchen, never put your knife inside the dishwashing area because others can get hurt.

Safety is always number one in a kitchen. Hold the knife close to yourself and keep the blade of the knife behind you and the tip of the knife pointed down. It's always better safe than sorry when holding and handling correctly and carrying so you can control the knife, and always keep in mind the amount you can carry before carrying the knife.

In addition, you must, when possible, put the knife on the table in order for the other person to remove it; it is much safer and is the safest way to give a person a knife. Also, knives are not to be played with because, as we all know, accidents can happen, and they surely do happen, and in order to avoid them, we don't play with knives in the kitchen.

Super Snacks and Berries

Why are berries among the healthiest of all foods? Is it because they are antioxidants? What is it that we know and don't know about fruits and berries?

dried goji berries
dried white mulberries
dried figs
dried apricots
dried papaya
dried plums
dried acai berries
dried cranberries

dried polar berries
dried golden berries
dried or fresh honeyberry aurora
gooseberries
miracle fruit
raspberries
strawberries
dried kiwis

Berries and their benefits

Acai berry: boost skin health, stimulates healthy digestion, high in antioxidants

Blackberry: promotes healthy hair, protects the heart, a source of potassium, and effective inflammatory

Bilberry: good for the eyes, rich in antioxidants, protects the liver and keeps the heart healthy

Blueberry: promotes eye health, can reduce belly fat, rich in antioxidants, and can aid digestion

Gooseberry: can reduce blood sugar, can improve eyesight, aids digestion, and promotes hair growth

Elderberry: energy booster, immune system booster, and an anti-inflammatory

Raspberry: can promote weight loss, good for bone health, and an antioxidant

Carbohydrates of vegetables and fruits

Artichoke	Apricot	Banana
Asparagus	Pomegranate	Grapefruit
Cranberries	Sweet potatoes	Eggplant
Beans	Avocado	Lemon
Cherries	Brussels sprouts	Peppers
Beets	Oranges	Honeydew
Passion fruit	Mushrooms	Purslane
Broccoli	Kale	Spinach
Cabbage	Spinach	Swiss chard
Cauliflower	Mustard greens	Zucchini
Collard greens	Parsnips	Yellow squash
Dandelion	Mango	Pears
Watermelon	Rutabaga	Fennel
Endive	Pineapple (in a	Lettuces
Guava	limited amount)	Papaya
Bell peppers	Parsley	Watercress
Plums	Kiwi	Cantaloupe
Carrots	Radish	Lychee
Celery	Seaweeds	Gooseberry
Cucumbers	Squash	Grapes
Green onion	Tomatillos	Figs
Onions	Turnips	
	Tomatoes	

Fats and healthy fats

Our introduction to fats or healthy fats is, in a lot of cases, the same, but we may write or read it the way we may want despite the way we would think or what we may do. In today's society, no matter how we think they may be, we all know we have good and bad fats.

Most importantly, to all who believe in healthy fats, we must have and maintain the right balance of fats we have in our diets.

In a vegan diet, you don't have as much fat as you do in a paleo diet. If on a paleo diet, your body is trained to burn fats instead of carbs for energy. The energy level in the paleo diet is more stable, and that is due to the way the paleo diet is structured.

Oils like coconut oil, avocado oils, and first pressed oils are always the best for vegan and paleo diets. Almond oils are good and are one of the healthy fats. In order to not chemically change our body's metabolism and to maintain our everyday diet, we should not skip those healthy fats in our meals.

What are the most known healthy fats

extra virgin olive oil	walnuts
avocado	macadamia nuts
raw almonds	organic peanut butter
pumpkin seeds	sunflower seeds,
egg yolks	vegetable oils
cashew	no name brand butter
walnuts	or peanut butter
organic butter	corn oil

Detoxifying and cleansing vegetables

Some people have problems and difficulties digesting dairy, but eliminating this could positively affect your body. But good news. Here are some of the detoxifying and cleaning vegetables that are good for us:

celery	cabbage
cucumbers	bok choy
cauliflower	broccoli
lettuce	kale
collard greens	arugula
beets	

If you like any of these items, you may eat as much as you would like. Some diets of vegan and paleo also include onions, spinach, and Brussels sprouts, and in some cases, you may add avocado. In some diets, you may also have asparagus, lots of garlic beets, grapefruits, artichokes, and ginger.

If at any time you wish for a snack for lunch, you may have pineapple chunks, celery sticks, grapefruit wedges, kiwi, or a banana.

There is much more to DCV. These are just a few of what we normally use today. As each country and culture has their way of cooking, we also have adapted their ways of not knowing. As the few times I was to Bosnia and Herzegovina, Split, and Croatia, I loved the full meat cuts and the bread baking. It was something that reminded me of back home, the way my sister would bake and the way one of my sisters would get up early in the morning and do the baking, or at a time, I would go to the slaughterhouse and buy the fresh cuts of beef to be cooked that day. We didn't need to refrigerate the meat because we cooked the meat just a couple of hours later. Where I come from, where it was a population of just under 1,400 inhabitants, there was cow-slaughtering two times a week, and there was no fresher meat that you could buy than the one that was slaughtered and then to watch the cow being cut in small pieces for sale.

Beets, cabbage, lettuce, and strawberries, along with white onions and other goodies, I would pick early in the morning in west of Frankfurt, Germany—something I would never forget, so many memories of cities and countries and good people I met along the way and people who cared and helped with the knowledge of what I have today. The last time I was in the Gambia, Africa, some good friends of mine told me about the benefits you can get from eating raw vegetable things I knew but didn't practice, but after all the schooling and the constant soaking my brain like a sponge from places and people I've talked to, that is what gives me the ability to write today. Also, I could remember picking fresh olives in Athens and Thessaloniki, something I enjoyed very much. And as a young boy, I would climb the avocado trees back home—time I remember like if it was yesterday, fruit as fresh as they come and as organic money can't buy.

Most Important Kitchen Methods

These are the methods we use each and every day in the kitchen but not in all because each method serves its own purpose; for example, poaching is to poach fish, pickling to pickle onions for later use, and steaming is to steam vegetables or dumplings.

broiling	baking
roasting	smoking
salting	frying
cooking	boiling
barbecuing	sautéing
kneading	toasting
grilling	poaching
creaming	flambéing
steaming	blanching
steeping	pickling

to baste, to baste a nice chicken breast after searing to sear

We also have some kitchens making their own fermentation and also growing good bacteria for foods.

Kitchen methods and techniques go a very long way and have no limits, no limits to practice, and no boundaries. Each country you go to, they have their own respective way of cooking, something we as cooks and chefs learn from every day because when we think we have it right, there is always somebody somewhere who is doing it differently. It does not always mean it's better, but it's different.

The Measurements

Cup	Fluid Ounce	Tablespoon	Teaspoon	Milliliter
1 c.	8 oz.	16 tbsp.	48 tsp.	237 ml.
3/2 c.	6 oz.	12 tbsp.	36 tsp.	177 ml.
2/3 c.	5 oz.	11 tbsp.	32 tsp.	158 ml.
1/2 c.	4 oz.	8 tbsp.	24 tsp.	118 ml.
1/3 c.	3 oz.	5 tbsp.	16 tsp.	79 ml.
1/4 c.	2 oz.	4 tbsp.	12 tsp.	59 ml.
1/8 c.	1 oz.	2 tbsp.	6 tsp.	30 ml.
1/16 c.	0.5 oz.	1 tbsp.	3 tsp.	15 ml.

Paleo and Vegan Side Dishes

Shredded Brussels Sprouts with Porcini or Champignon Mushrooms

1–2 portions

This is a wonderful dish, either eaten as a side order on top of a salad or as a salad. It is perfect for all you vegans and vegetarians who enjoy a no-meat product and a dairy-free product.

1/2 lb. sliced mushrooms
1 lb. shredded Brussels sprouts
1 tbsp. chopped garlic
4 tbsp. chopped white onions
4 tbsp. chopped parsley
1/2 tsp. salt
1/2 tsp. ground black pepper
6 tbsp. extra virgin olive oil
Preheat oven to 350° F 15 minutes before baking.

Heat a sauté pan on medium to high heat, then add the oil, onions, and garlic. Sauté for 2 minutes. Add the mushrooms and the shredded Brussels sprouts. Cook for about 5 minutes. In a preheated oven on a sheet pan, add the mixture to the sheet pan and bake for 15 minutes. Thereafter, remove from oven and allow to cool before refrigerating or serving at one.

Roasted Butternut Squash

2–3 portions

For all you who enjoy vegan food, this is for you, and it's also perfect for all you who may have celiac disease but who also enjoys roasted root vegetables.

4 c. chopped butternut squash, cut in cubes (optional)
1/2 c. golden raisins
4 tbsp. chopped parsley
6 tbsp. vegetable or olive oil
1/2 tbsp. salt
4–6 tbsp. cinnamon syrup
Preheat oven to 325° F.

In a bowl, combine the butternut squash oil and salt then place on a sheet pan or baking pan with parchment paper roast in the oven for about 40 minutes, turning every 15 minutes until tender but firm to the touch. Remove from oven. When finished, mix with cinnamon syrup, parsley, and golden raisins. You may serve hot or cold.

Cinnamon syrup

1/2 c. sugar (1/2 c. honey if using for paleo)
1 c. water
1/4 tsp. powdered cinnamon
2 cinnamon sticks (optional)
1 tbsp. juniper berries (optional)

In cooking small to medium, add sugar, water, cinnamon sticks, and berries. Allow to cook until syrup forms and is light in color.

Reduce by half or cook to one-fourth liquid. I like to add the berries to the syrup in order to change the flavor. A chef in Madrid used the juniper berries because he thought the syrup would not be boring.

When using honey and cinnamon powder, the substance will be looser. Keep in mind that for paleo, no sugar can be used, but real bee honey should then be substituted for the sugar.

Roasted Collard Greens

3–4 portions

Collard greens are very healthy. Either blanched, roasted, or braised, they are healthy.

11/2 lb. fresh collard greens
6 tbsp. olive oil
1 tsp. kosher salt
1 tsp. ground white pepper
6 tbsp. to 1/4 c. vegetable broth
1/4 c. diced yellow onions
1/4 tsp. cumin
1/4 tsp. ground dried garlic or garlic flakes

Take the collard greens and wash them chorally. If needed, triple wash because, at times, they look clean but could still have sand in between. Remove the string from the middle of the leave and thread by cutting at about 1/4 inch in wide.

Heat a sauté pan on medium to high heat and sauté the collard green seasoning as you go. At the end of the cookery, with all the collard greens cooked in a pan, add the onions and cook for 2 minutes. Then add the broth and cumin. Serve hot or cold with other accompaniments as a salad.

Paleo and Vegan Dishes

Spaghetti Squash Lasagna

3–4 portions

Using spaghetti squash as a substitute is the most and healthiest choice that can be made. You may also use zucchini noodles made from zucchini and yellow squash.

1.5 lb. spaghetti squash (about 3 lb. spaghetti squash)
1 lb. mild Italian sausage
1 c. diced Spanish onions
1 tbsp. dried basil
1.5 c. pizza sauce, sugar-free
2 whole eggs, whisks and set to the side
8×8 baking pan
Preheat oven to 375° F 15 minutes before.

Wash and cut the squash side down. On a sheet baking pan, grease the baking pan with 1 tablespoon of olive oil and bake for 30 minutes. Reduce oven temperature to 325 degrees and bake for an additional 10 minutes. Remove from oven and then remove threads and place in a cooking pot on medium heat. Add Italian sliced sausage and onions and cook for 10 minutes. Add pizza sauce and dried basil. Mix well and season to taste with salt and fresh ground black pepper. With the spaghetti squash, add the egg mixture to the squash and mix well. Now add to the 8×8 baking pan and bake for 45 minutes to an hour at 350 degrees. Remove from oven and allow to rest for 30 minutes before serving.

Paleo/Keto Beef Stroganoff

4–5 portions

In this recipe, you don't necessarily need to eat it with pasta or potatoes. You can eat it with steamed vegetables or sweet potatoes. You may also make a nice spaghetti squash and eat it with that. Spaghetti squash is healthy and nice when made and served with a little olive oil and chopped parsley.

2 lb. cubed beef
1 lb. chopped cremini or shiitake or white button mushrooms
1/2 c. arrowroot mix with one cup water
4–6 tbsp. olive oil
1.5 c. diced white or yellow onions
4 tbsp. chopped fresh garlic
1/2 tbsp. coriander
2 tbsp. salt
1/2 tbsp. ground white pepper
1/4 tbsp. rosemary
1/4 tbsp. celery seeds (optional)
4–6 c. water or beef broth

In a large pot, add olive oil on high heat. Add cubed beef and brown for about 5 to 7 minutes. Add onions and garlic. Cook for 15 minutes. Then add 2 cups of water or beef broth. Cook for an additional 10 minutes on medium heat. Add salt, pepper, coriander, and rosemary and simmer for 20 minutes, adding 1/2 cup water or broth every 10 minutes. Add mushrooms and cook for 15 minutes on high heat. Now you may add the arrowroot mix and simmer for 10 minutes. Meat should be nice, tender, and tasty. Serve with any sides you may like.

Haricot Vert Roasted with Almonds

3–4 portions

String beans (specialty green beans)—these are French green beans. We usually use string beans that almost have the same taste but are more decorative and more luxurious in color and texture.

1.5 lb. haricot vert (blanched)
1 c. diced white or yellow Spanish onions
6 tbsp. olive oil
1 c. roasted sliced almonds
Salt and pepper to taste
Large pot of boiling water
Large pot with cold water and ice and a strainer or sieve
Preheat oven to 350° F.

On a sheet pan or in a baking pan, place the almonds in the preheated oven and roast the almonds for about 5 to 10 minutes in the oven, moving every couple of minutes until golden brown. Remove from oven and set to the side.

In a large pot with boiling water, blanch the haricot vert or beans for 30 seconds. From hot water, transfer to the cold water using the sieve and cool down the beans in just a minute until beans are bright and green. Drain or pat dry. In a sauté pan, add 4 tablespoons of oil and caramelize the onions cooking for about 5 to 10 minutes on medium heat. Set to the side. Add 2 tablespoons of oil and roast the haricot vert or beans in two batches, roasting in the pan on high heat for 2 minutes. In a large bowl, add the haricot vert, caramelized onions, almonds and season with salt and pepper. Serve cold or hot.

Beef Brisket with Root Vegetables

4–6 orders

With this recipe, you can either use brisket flank steak or skirt steak. They both will work the same. In some cases, skirts steak works much better if cooked on high flame when the brisket is either braised or baked.

3–5 lb. of brisker (grass-fed preferably)
1/2 c. olive oil for the veggies
6 tbsp. honey

Mixture
1/2 tbsp. curry powder
1/2 tsp. ground ginger
6 tbsp. olive oil
1 tbsp. celery seeds
1 tbsp. minced rosemary
1/2 tsp. ground cinnamon
1/4 tsp. black pepper
1 tsp. salt

Veggies for braising
1 c. chopped white onions
1/2 lb. sliced carrots (peeled)
1 lb. chopped celery
1/2 lb. sliced parsnips (peeled)
1 lb. cubed sweet potato (peeled)
4 tbsp. chopped garlic
1.5 c. coconut milk (canned)
1 c. red wine (optional)

2–4 c. beef broth

Preheat oven to 375° F.

In a small to medium bowl, add the cinnamon powder, ginger powder, olive oil, curry powder, celery seeds, along with the salt and pepper, and mix well. Rub the mixture on the brisket and place it in the oven in a medium to large pan or pot.

In a large bowl, mix the vegetables, along with the olive oil, and braise in the oven in a baking pan at 350 degrees for 20 to 25 minutes. Now add 1 cup of beef broth, coconut milk, honey, and garlic. Bake for 15 minutes before adding to the brisket. Bake for an additional 25 to 30 minutes, checking every 10 to 15 minutes until brisket is nice and tender. Add the rest of the coconut milk and broth. Allow the brisket to sit for about 20 to 30 minutes before serving.

Brussels Sprouts and Bacon Bites

3–4 portions

Brussels sprouts are one of my favorite vegetables when done the right way. Not everybody can bake, roast, or blanch Brussels sprouts, but they are very good for you.

    1.5 lb. Brussels sprouts cut in half
    8–10 tbsp. olive oil
    1/4 tsp. nutmeg
    1 tbsp. salt
    1/2 tbsp. black pepper
    1/2 c. bacon bites ready cooked (optional)
    1/2 c. bacon sliced and cooked
    6 tbsp. chopped parsley
    1/4 tsp. garlic powder or granulated
    Preheat oven to 375° F.

Wash and cut Brussels sprouts in half. Then add to a large bowl and mix with the nutmeg, salt, pepper, garlic powder, and oil. On a sheet pan with parchment paper, place the Brussels sprouts in the oven and roast for 10 minutes. Lower the oven temperature to 350 degrees and bake for an additional 12 minutes; rotate of mix in order for even roasting. If needed, bake for an additional few minutes if not tender enough. Professionally, Brussels sprouts are nice if crunchy and are very tasty. Serve as a side dish or accompanied with other foods.

Roasted Cauliflower with Garlic

2–4 portions

This roasted cauliflower dish is very tasty, especially if you are vegan. Cauliflower is very healthy and is used as rice in many restaurants after it was discovered by many that it could be used as rice and for stuffing. The cauliflower is very simple, very healthy, and quick to prepare.

1 2.5 lb. cauliflower cut in florets
1/4 to 1/2 c. olive oil
1 tbsp. salt
1/4 tbsp. fresh ground white pepper
2 tbsp. chopped or minced garlic
2–4 tbsp. chopped parsley
1/4 tsp. ground nutmeg (optional)
Preheat oven to 350° F.

Clean of stems and wash the cauliflower. Now cut in bite-size pieces. Place in a bowl, along with the olive oil, salt, and pepper with minced or chopped garlic. Mix well and put on a baking sheet pan and bake in the oven at 375 degrees for 10 minutes. Turn sheet pan around and bake for an additional 5 to 10 minutes. Remove from oven and mix with chopped parsley. Serve.

Baked Organic or Freshwater Salmon

2–4 portions

This salmon recipe I've done over and over again for so many people, and the plate is always clean because it's so healthy, simple, and quick. Not much prep is needed. The first time I prepared, the salmon was for about 2,500 people. The prep was done with about seven prep cooks at a gala in Vienna, Austria, where I was working as a banquet chef and in Frankfurt as a Bruch chef. Things were kind of work different in Europe than here at home, and it was done again at a sport and press ball in Frankfurt, Germany, for another 1,400 people.

4 4–6 oz. pieces of salmon filets (no bones)
10 1/4 in. sliced of zucchini cut in half moon
10 1/4 in. sliced of yellow squash cut in half moon
2 c. chopped Spanish onions
1/2 c. olive oil
2 tbsp. chopped fresh garlic
4 tbsp. chopped parsley
2–4 tbsp. celery seed (optional)
Preheat the oven to 375° F 10–15 minutes before baking time.

Take the zucchini and yellow squash. Wash and slice them on a slicer, or you may also slice them with your knife. Slice the yellow squash and zucchini in slices and then across in half moon. Then set to the side. On medium heat in a small pot, cook the onions and garlic with 4 tablespoons olive oil with the garlic for about 5 minutes, stirring, making sure the onions and garlic do not burn. Add the parsley and set it to the side. On a baking pan, place the salmon and decorate the salmon with the zucchini and yellow squash—green then yellow, green then yellow. Salt and pepper the veggies and bake in the oven for about 10 to 17 minutes, depending on if you like your salmon somewhat pink or well cooked. Myself working at banquets, buffets, and ala cart, I find people they all eat differently—some like salmon well done and others pink. It doesn't matter. After salmon is baked, remove from oven and serve with the onion and garlic mixture. Serve either hot or warm with your choice of sides.

Bruschetta Spread

2–4 portions

This lovely topping is something I had at a convention in Chios (Xios), Greece, one of the many conventions I visited for about five years. That supposed to be Italian bruschetta is served in many different ways. I hope this will be something you enjoy the way I do. You don't have to spread this mixture on a baguette but on grilled portobello mushroom. In that way, vegan, vegetarian, and keto dieters can have this fun topping.

1.5 c. chopped (diced) plum tomatoes about 1 lb.
1 tbsp. minced fresh garlic
2 tbsp. balsamic vinegar
4–6 tbsp. extra virgin olive oil
6 freshly chopped or sliced basil leaves
1 tbsp. salt or 1 tsp.
1 tsp. ground black pepper
4–6 tbsp. crumbled feta cheese (optional)
2 tbsp. chopped green olives (optional)

Wash tomatoes, take out the seeds, dice the tomatoes, then set to the side. Take 2 to 3 cloves of garlic peel and dice. Then add to the diced tomatoes. Add the garlic balsamic vinegar and olive oil to the tomatoes. Season to taste with salt and pepper. Then add the sliced basil. Feta cheese and olives are optional. If adding the olives and cheese, please use 1 teaspoon because you will have enough salt.

You may use it on a toasted baguette of baked or grilled portobello mushrooms.

Red Cabbage Confit

3–5 portions

In this recipe, I am not asking for a specified red wine because, at times, you don't or can't find a nice cooking red wine. I usually use a nice red wine reduced until it thickens. I cool this confit because of the way it's made and the ingredients it has. It is similar to a red beet soup.

This red cabbage reminds me of winters in Austria and Germany, where I would go to the Weihnachtenmark to drink glühwein. This recipe has no citrus like the glühwein, but it still reminds me of it.

1 4–5 lb. red cabbage
6 c. red wine (optional)
6 c. red cooking wine
1.5 tbsp. juniper berries
1/4 tsp. cloves (optional)
2 tbsp. butter or 4 tbsp. olive oil
2 c. cold water
4 tbsp. honey
1 tbsp. salt
1 tsp. salt
2 c. diced onions
2 c. chopped green apples

In a separate pot, add the wine and reduce it by half on medium to high heat (wine reduction). Wash, shred, or rough chop the red cabbage. Place in a large cooking pot with the butter or olive oil and cook on high heat for 5 to 10 minutes, constantly stirring. Allow to cook until tender or firm to the touch. It will take about 25 to 30 minutes at most. Serve hot or cold as a side order or accompanied with something else.

Add the onions and juniper berries, along with the honey, salt, and pepper. Now add the reduced red wine and apples and cook for 5 minutes before adding the water.

Avocado and Hard-Boiled Egg Salad

3–5 portions

With this salad, it can be used to mixed in with salad greens. Use a spread or a stuffing for ripe plum tomatoes or avocado with shrimps or lobster. I made some small changes to the recipe after eating at a hotel in Dubai, but trust it will be just as good with the small changes I made.

2 to 3 ripe avocados
6 tbsp. chopped red onions
2 tbsp. sliced chives
4 tbsp. fresh lemon juice
4 tbsp. olive oil
6 tbsp. white wine vinegar
4 hard-boiled eggs, boil the eggs for about 12 minutes
1/2 cup mayonnaise (optional)
4 tbsp. plain yogurt (optional)
2 tbsp. sour cream (optional)
1/2 tbsp. salt
1 tsp. white ground pepper
1/4 tsp. pink corn pepper

This recipe is for those who can't have dairy. For the recipe with yogurt and sour cream, you don't need mayonnaise and the other way around. With the no-dairy salad, you may use olive oil and vinegar. In the below description is the use of olive oil and vinegar.

Cut and remove the avocado seed. Cut into bite-size pieces and mix with the lemon juice and set to the side. Peel and chop the hard-boiled eggs. Then add to the avocado mix gently and season with salt and white ground pepper. Personally, I don't like runny eggs but have made them locally and professionally for others. In a separate bowl, mix the olive oil, chives, and white wine vinegar. Add the dressing to the avocado and egg mixture, along with scallions, chives, salt, and pepper. Mix gently together. Serve cold as a plum tomato stuffing avocado stuffing or on a nicely grilled portobello mushroom.

Cauliflower Mint and Strawberry Salad

2–4 portions

This salad is light and tasty. It's also flavorful. The cauliflower can be either steamed, roasted, or blanched. In this recipe, the cauliflower is to be blanched and put in an ice bath.

    1.5 lb. cauliflower florets
    1 lb. fresh strawberries
    1 c. frozen strawberries
    1 c. olive
    1/2 c. apple cider vinegar or tarragon vinegar
    2 tbsp. mustard
    1 tsp. poppy seeds
    1/4 tbsp. salt and pepper
    1.5 tbsp. honey
    4–6 fresh mint leaves
    1 large bowl with an ice bath

In a large pot of boiling water, blanch the cauliflower florets for about 1 minute. Remove the florets and transfer them to the ice bath. Remove from the ice bath and allow to drain dry. In a blender, place half the frozen strawberries and blend on medium, adding the vinegar oil and mustard. Now add the rest of the strawberries, along with mint leaves, honey, poppy seeds, salt, and pepper and set to the side. Wash and cut the strawberries in four. In a large bowl, add the cauliflower and sliced strawberries and dress with the dressing. Serve at once or place in the refrigerator.

Luscious Cod or Tilapia

4–6 portions

This cod/tilapia recipe came on one of my visits to Brussels, Belgium. In the city of Belgium, they have some of the restaurants that serve on the outside, something you don't see too often in NYC, but it was great. During the time I lived in Brussels, I made friends with a few chefs and got to know some of the owners because a friend of mine, Francias, from Brussels, they were friends of him, but the recipe was given to me, and I made some changes of my own.

3 lb. cod or tilapia filet
6 tbsp. olive oil
3 tbsp. capers
1/2 c. diced white onions
3 tbsp. minced garlic
3 tbsp. chopped flat parsley
1/2 c. white wine
4 tbsp. olive oil
1/3 c. almond cream (use if paleo) or 1/2 c. coconut milk
Freshly ground white pepper and a touch of salt

When cooking paleo, you may use butter. Vegan is no dairy or animal product, so omit the olive oil. In a sauté pan, heat olive oils and sear the cod or tilapia on both sides for 3 to 4 minutes. Sear the cod or tilapia 3 to 4 pieces at a time. When all done, remove and set to the side. Then add the onions and garlic and cook for 3 minutes on medium to high heat. Add the wine and cook for an additional 2–4 minutes. Add the fish to the sauce, along with the capers and chopped parsley. Season salt and freshly ground white pepper. Please keep in mind the capers are salty and may not need too much. If cooking as paleo, you may add butter and heavy cream. This dish tastes beautiful when blended with roasted potatoes and steamed vegetables. You may also serve the finished fish on a bed of lettuce or in a salad with a salad dressing of your choice.

Paleo Meatballs

Curry Pork Meatballs

2–4 portions

These pork meatballs can be served as an ordinary meal or as paleo, along with nicely made cauliflower rice simply seasoned with olive oil, salt, pepper, and maybe a little chopped parsley. Pork meatballs can also be substituted for bison. For those who are not too fond of pork, you can have bison or a mixture of beef and bison. These pork meatballs made with a coconut cream curry sauce is a marriage made in your mouth. A part of my specialty is coconut and curry, something I'm working on at the moment for my next upcoming fusion cookbook.

    1.5 lb. ground pork
    1/4 tbsp. ground coriander
    3 tbsp. chopped cilantro
    2 whole eggs
    4–6 tbsp. olive oil
    1/3 c. minced garlic
    1/2 c. minced white onions
    1/2 tbsp. ground black pepper
    1/2 tbsp. kosher salt
    1/4 tsp. cumin
    1/2 c. oatmeal (optional)
    1/2 c. almond flour (optional)

Sauce
    2 c. coconut milk
    1 tbsp. olive oil
    1 tbsp. minced garlic
    2 tbsp. diced white onions

4 tbsp. chopped cilantro
2 tbsp. sour cream or cream of coconut
1/2 tbsp. cumin
1/2 tsp. cayenne pepper
1/2 tsp. crushed red pepper
1 tbsp. minced garlic
Salt and pepper

In a bowl, combine ground meat and dry ingredients. Add eggs (optional) and mix. Now form meatballs to 1/4 ounce meatballs.

In a sauté pan, add the olive oil and brown the meatballs. Cook on each side for about 2 to 3 minutes on medium to high heat. Then set them to the side.

In a separate saucepan, heat oil and then add the onions and garlic and cook for about 2 minutes. Add the coconut milk and cook for 5 minutes on medium heat. Now add the dry ingredients and cook for an additional 5 minutes. Add the cream of coconut and reduce the cream by 1/3 season with salt and cook for 3 more minutes or until thickened. Add the meatballs to the sauce and serve hot or cold.

Roasted Arugula and Carrots

2–4 portions

This recipe was discovered at a gala some time ago when I was working for Kafers, a company based out of Wiesbaden, Germany. I was working with lovely people, people who showed me a lot of what I know today.

2 lb. carrots peeled and cut on the bias 1/4 inch
4 c. fresh arugula
2 tbsp. fennels seeds
1/4 tbsp. celery seeds
4 tbsp. olive oil
4 tbsp. olive oil for arugula
1 tbsp. minced or diced garlic for arugula
3 tbsp. of chopped white onions for arugula
1 tsp. salt
1/2 tsp. peppers
1 tbsp. chopped or minced garlic
1/4 tsp. cumin (optional)
Preheat the oven to 375° F for 15 minutes.

In a large bowl, combine the carrots, olive oil, salt, pepper, and fennel seeds. Place on a sheet pan or baking pan with parchment paper. Turn oven down to 350 degrees and bake for 20 minutes. Turn the pan around and mix the carrots to have them evenly bake. Bake for another 15 minutes. In a sauté pan, add the oil and garlic and cook on high heat for 3 minutes. Add the arugula a little at a time, cooking and constantly stirring for about 3 minutes. When done, add to the finished carrots and serve as a side, or you may have it as a vegan dish.

Avocado Quinoa with Grilled Chicken

2–4 portions

This quinoa avocado dish can be eaten either cold or hot. Personally, I like it if the quinoa is eaten warm.

Cook the quinoa separately and grain in a strainer.

1/2 c. red quinoa
1/2 c. white quinoa
4 c. water
1 tsp. lemon zest
4 tbsp. dice white onions
2 tbsp. olive oil
2 tbsp. thinly sliced scallions
Salt and pepper
2 fresh lemons squeezed

In a medium pot on medium to high heat, add oil, onions, and quinoa. Cook for 2 minutes. Then add lemon zest and cook for 8 to 12 minutes. Remove from heat and pass through a strainer. Then set aside.

Peal in quarters 4 avocados and chop in bite-size pieces.

1/2 c. chopped cilantro
1/4 c. olive oil
1/2 c. red peppers
1/4 c. chickpeas
1.5 c. chopped grilled chicken

In a large bowl, combine the quinoa, avocado, and fresh lemon juice. Mix and season with salt and pepper. Add remaining ingredients. Serve with warm quinoa or cold quinoa.

Grilled Avocado with Spicy Chicken

2–4 portions

This grilled avocado is on the higher end of cuisine and cooking. As I was training at a tapas place in Spain a few years ago, I made this dish, but it is different. I rewrote the recipe with a different twist and flavor even if I've seen this form of an avocado recipe in Europe and also in Dubai.

> 2 avocados
> 2 tbsp. fresh lemon juice
> 1/4 tsp. salt and pepper
> 1 tbsp. olive oil

On an open-flame grill, brush the avocado with olive oil and grill for 2 to 3 minutes on each side. Season with salt and pepper and brush with lemon juice. Now set to the side.

Grilled chicken
> 1 lb. raw shredded or diced chicken
> 2 tbsp. chopped cilantro
> 1 tbsp. salt and pepper
> 1 tbsp. chopped fresh garlic
> 2 tbsp. chopped or diced tomatoes, no seeds
> 1 tbsp. diced red bell peppers
> 2 tbsp. chopped jalapeno peppers
> 1/4 tbsp. cayenne powder
> 4 tbsp. olive oil
> Turn the grill on.

In a sauté pan, add 2 tablespoons olive oil and cook the tomatoes with pepper and season with salt and peppers for 3 minutes. In a bowl, combine chicken oil, garlic, and cilantro and cook on the grill for 5 to 8 minutes. After the chicken is cooked, combine in a bowl, along with the cooked peppers and tomatoes. Stuff the grilled avocado with the cooked chicken and pepper mixture. Serve avocado as a side or main entrée dish.

Cactus with Diced Tomatoes

2–4 portions

This light vegan dish was crafted, developed, and written after I was on a trip to Tijuana, Mexico. I had this, along with "cotija," which I omitted from the diced or grated plain roasted coconut recipe.

    1.5 lb. prickly pear fruit cactus
    1/2 c. diced tomatoes
    1/2 chopped and sliced Spanish onions
    2 tbsp. chopped
    1/2 c. shaved, diced, or crumbled roasted coconut
    1/2 c. diced grilled or roasted chicken

Either you can buy the cactus cleaned, or you can clean and cut yourself. Shave or cut the prickles of the eatable cactus and cut them into bite-size pieces.

    1 c. vinaigrette
    1/2 c. olive oil
    4 tbsp. white or red vinegar
    1/4 tbsp. lime juice
    1 tsp. minced garlic

In a small bowl, combine the oil and vinegar with the minced garlic, along with the lime juice and vinaigrette. Season with salt and pepper.

Marinade for chicken
    1/2 lb. chicken breast or thigh
    1 tbsp. minced garlic

1 tbsp. chopped cilantro
2 tbsp. water
1/2 tbsp. onion powder
1 tbsp. sweet paprika
1/4 tsp. salt
1/2 tbsp. ground black pepper

In a bowl, combine chicken and all ingredients and marinate for about an hour before grilling. Grill chicken on both sides for about 2 to 4 minutes, turning until finish.

In a large bowl, combine the cactus chicken, along with the chopped tomatoes, onions, and coconut, with the vinaigrette and the slice of diced chicken. Serve at once with your choice of side.

Sweet Potato Hash

2–4 portions

After making some changes, I decided to write this one recipe after making the necessary changes. Please make sure when you buy sweet potatoes, they are the pink meat potatoes because they cook much better than the white meat sweet potatoes. In some places, you will see them as yams or sweet potatoes. If you buy yams, they can be white or pink meat, but if you buy sweet potatoes, they will be pink meat.

    1.5 lb. sweet potatoes
    1/2 c. olive oil
    4 tbsp. chopped parsley
    1 tsp. salt
    1 tsp. ground black pepper
    1 tbsp. chopped or minced garlic
    4 tbsp. minced or diced white onions
    2 tbsp. sliced scallions
    4 tbsp. sundried cranberries (optional)

In a large sauté pan, heat some of the oil and sauté a little of the potatoes at the time in just about four stages. In separate frying or sauté pan, sauté the onions and garlic for 2–3 minutes, along with the scallions and cranberries.

Sauté the potatoes. Once done, transfer to a large pot with the onions and scallion mixture. Season with salt and pepper. Serve as is or as aside. Serve hot.

Roasted Bok Choy with Bacon

2–4 portion

This recipe was changed just a bit from sesame oil and seeds, and it was also changed from a steamed and wood-roasted duck. It is still tasty and pleasant to eat and enjoy. If you like a duck, you may add duck, but you will not find roasted or steamed duck in the book.

6–8 heads of baby bok choy
2 c. thick-cut cured bacon
1/2 c. sliced scallions
1/4 tsp. crushed red pepper flakes
3 tbsp. minced or chopped garlic
2 tbsp. chopped fresh ginger
6 tbsp. olive oil
1 tbsp. orange zest
Fresh ground pepper and kosher salt

Under cold water, slice the bok choy lengthwise by half an inch. Wash, clean, and set to the side and allow to drain. In a sauté pan on medium to high heat, cook the bacon until crispy in batches and set to the side. Use the leftover bacon fat to sauté the bok choy. In a pan on medium heat, sauté the bok choy in three stages, adding a little ginger and garlic a little at the same time seasoning with salt and pepper. You may use a tablespoon or two of water if needed to cook the bok choy. When all done, combine the bacon and bok choy in a large sauté pan or cooking pot. Serve at once.

Quinoa and Grilled Chicken Salad

2–4 portions

With this quinoa dish, I first had quinoa in 2002 back in Ecuador, one of the first times I visited for the first time on the kind of business trip I made for some friends in NYC.

Cooking quinoa
- 1.5 c. quinoa
- 1 tbsp. olive oil
- 1 tbsp. lemon or orange zest
- 1 tsp. mixture of salt and pepper
- 3 c. water

In a cooking pot on medium to high heat, add the quinoa, water, lemon zest, oil, salt, and pepper. Cook for 15 to 20 minutes or until 3/4 inches of water is left in the pot. Remove from the stove and set to the side and passed through a strainer.

Salad ingredients
- 1 avocado, sliced or diced
- 1.5 c. arugula
- 1.5 c. mixed greens
- 1 whole tomato diced seeds removed
- 1/2 c. sliced carrots
- 4 tbsp. sliced scallions
- 3 c. grilled chicken
- 1/2 c. diced cucumber
- 4 tbsp. diced red onions
- 2 whole hard-boiled eggs, sliced

Salad dressing
> 2 tbsp. lemon juice
> 1/2 c. olive oil
> 1/4 c. red wine vinegar
> 1 tbsp. minced shallots
> 1 tbsp. mustard
> 1 tbsp. minced red onions
> 1 tbsp. hone (optional)

In a small bowl, add all ingredients and whisk until dressing consistency. You may add 2 tablespoons of chopped parsley to the salad dressing if you like. In a large bowl, add ingredients gently. Add dressing individually as needed in order not for the salad to become soggy. Serve at once or refrigerate until needed.

Sweet Potato Salad

2–4 portions

This sweet potato salad has been changed around a little. I made a few substitutes in order to accommodate it for vegan or paleo. Originally, it was a trio potato salad, along with a few ingredients that didn't represent paleo or vegan.

    2 lb. sweet potatoes
    1/2 c. sliced scallions
    1/2 c. sundried cranberries
    1 c. arugula
    1 c. baby spinach
    1/2 c. thinly sliced red onions
    1/2 c. pomegranates
    1 c. roasted cauliflower

Roasting cauliflower
    Cut half of the cauliflower into bite-size pieces.

    1/2 tsp. curry powder
    1/2 tsp. cumin powder
    1/2 tsp. salt and pepper
    4 tbsp. olive oil

In a bowl, combine all five ingredients and bake on a sheet pan in a preheated oven at 375 degrees for 20 minutes. Remove from oven and allow to cool down.

Roasting sweet potatoes
    Peel and cut sweet potatoes in 1/2 inch squares.

4 tbsp. olive oil
1 tsp. salt and pepper
Preheat oven to 375° F for about 10 minutes.

In a large bowl, combine sweet potatoes, salt, pepper, and olive oil. Mix and place on a sheet pan lined with parchment paper. Place in oven and bake for 15 minutes. Turn the pan around and bake for an additional 20 minutes or until tender and brown. Remove from oven and set to the side on a cooling rack or in a cool place. Keep it simple and fresh.

Spicy Chicken and Sprouts

4–6 orders

This spicy chicken and sprouts recipe is originally made with a few other ingredients, including feta cheese, but because it has to be made for paleo and vegan, I needed to make some changes in the structure of the ingredients and the balance of the recipe.

1 lb. plump chicken breast cut in small cubes
1/2 c. sliced scallions
1 lb. Brussels sprouts, shredded
1/2 c. chopped parsley
1/2 cup chopped cilantro
6–8 tbsp. olive oil
1 tbsp. sweet paprika
1 tsp. cayenne pepper
1 tbsp. granulated garlic
1 tsp. onion powder

Take the Brussels sprouts and wash them. Then cut them in half and allow them to drain for 10 minutes. In the meantime, turn on the oven to 375 degrees for 10 to 15 minutes. In a medium bowl, mix the Brussels sprouts with salt and pepper, along with 5 table-spoons olive oil. Place on a sheet pan and roast in the oven for 15 minutes. On the stovetop, heat the rest of the oil in a sauté pan. Add the cubed chicken and roast for 3 minutes on medium to high heat. Now remove the Brussels sprouts from the oven. Turn oven down to 300 degrees. Now add the chicken to the sprouts and the parsley. Chopped cilantro and place in the oven and bake for an additional 5 minutes. Season with kosher salt and white pepper. Serve at once. You may enjoy hot or cold.

Southwestern Beef and Rice

2–5 portions

This lovely high-protein paleo keto dish is perfect for a picnic park lunch break or even after your workout before dinner. You may also have this for dinner, along with the rice and your choice of vegetables.

1/2 c. diced onions
3 tbsp. chopped fresh garlic
1 tbsp. paprika powder
1 tsp. granulated onions
1 lb. lean ground beef
4 tbsp. tomato paste
1 c. canned crush tomatoes
1 tsp. ground cumin
2 tbsp. olive oil
4 tbsp. diced carrots
4 tbsp. diced celery
1/2 tsp. cayenne pepper
Salt and pepper

In a large saucepan, add the oil and height for 1 minute on medium to high heat. Add ground beef, onions, and celery and cook for 4 minutes. Now add the tomato paste and crushed tomatoes, along with the seasoning, and cook for 5 to 8 minutes. Stir with a wooden spoon and cook for an additional 5 minutes on medium heat. Set to the side.

Rice/cauliflower rice
1 cauliflower cut in large cubes or 4 c.
4 tbsp. diced onions

4 tbsp. olive oil
4 tbsp. chopped parsley
4 tbsp. diced zucchini
4 tbsp. chopped fresh garlic
Kosher salt and white ground pepper

Wash and cut the cauliflower into cubes. In the food processor, add the cauliflower and chop the cauliflower like rice consistency. After blended, place a cooking pan on medium heat with the olive oil and cook the cauliflower rice in two batches, along with onions, zucchini, and fresh garlic. Season with salt and white pepper with the southwestern beef hot or at room temperature.

Stuffed Zucchini Boats

4–6 portions

This recipe should make your mouth water. It's delicious, tasty, and special, and the stuffing can be used in stuffing tomatoes, plantains, turkey, or in your Christmas ham.

4 medium-size zucchini, cut in half and scoop out the inside
1/2 lb. ground pork
1/2 lb. ground beef
1/2 c. diced celery
1/2 diced green peppers
4 tbsp. chopped cilantro
1 tsp. cayenne pepper
1 tsp. granulated garlic
1/2 tsp. cumin
1 tbsp. paprika
1/2 tsp. black pepper
1 tbsp. kosher salt
1/2 c. currants
4 tbsp. olive oil
6 tbsp. chopped fresh parsley
1 c. crushed tomatoes
1/2 tsp. dried or fresh thyme
4 tbsp. tomato paste
Turn on the oven and heat at 350° F.

Grease a baking or sheet pan with olive oil and bake the zucchini boats for 7 minutes. Remove from the oven and set to the side. Wash zucchinis and cut in half lengthwise, scooping out the middle part, making room for the stuffing. In a large pot, add the olive oil, along with the ground beef and ground pork. Cook for 4 to 7 minutes. Gradually add the crushed tomatoes and tomato paste, along with the celery, and cook for 5 minutes on medium to high heat. Add the seasoning and cook for an additional 6 minutes. Add the parsley and cilantro and turn off the heat. Spoon the cooked product into the zucchini boats and bake for 8 minutes in a 375 degree oven. Remove when done and serve at once. You may also enjoy it at room temperature.

Roasted Marble Sweet Potatoes

2–4 portions

With this roasted sweet potato recipe, you will see it's for everybody, young and old vegetarian, paleo, or vegan. I hope you enjoy these potatoes as much as I do and as much as the people I made them for. Every time I made these for friends, they enjoyed them and wanted more.

> 2.5 lb. of cubed sweet potatoes
> 6 tbsp. olive oil
> 3 tbsp. granulated garlic
> 2 tbsp. diced fresh garlic
> 1 tbsp. kosher salt
> 1 tsp. ground white peppers
> 1 tbsp. kosher salt

Mixture
> 2 c. diced Spanish onions
> 1/2 c. finely sliced scallions
> 4 tbsp. chopped parsley
> 2 tbsp. chopped cilantro
> 1 tsp. ground black pepper
> 6 tbsp. olive oil
> 4 tbsp. sundried cranberries
> Preheat the oven to 375° F for 15 minutes and then lower to 350° F.

In a large bowl, combine the sweet potatoes, granulated and fresh garlic, olive oil, salt, and pepper in the bowl. On a sheet pan or baking pan, place the potatoes and bake for 10 minutes. Mix the potatoes after 10 minutes and roast for another 15 minutes at 350 degrees. In the meantime, on the stovetop in a sauté pan, heat the oil and caramelize the onions, constantly stirring until brown on medium to high heat. After caramelizing, add the scallions, parsley, cilantro, and black pepper. Remove the roasted sweet potatoes from the oven and mix in a bowl the onions and cranberry mixture. Serve at once or at room temperature.

Paleo and Keto Chicken

3–5 portions

Preparing and cooking this recipe reminds me of cooking onboard a river cruise yacht back in Europe some years ago. At the time, it was not clear to me the difference between keto and paleo and why so many people would order this chicken because the customers would have the choice of either chicken beef or fish, a common way of ordering if there is a limit on what you can order. Just lie onboard an aircraft if you're flying coach, all you can order is either chicken, beef, or fish, and that is practically the same way it is on those cruises. But for whatever reason, the passengers would order this chicken dish 70 percent of the time, and if it was a long four- to seven-day cruise, this is what they would order.

2 lb. skinless and boneless chicken breast
1/2 c. sliced scallions
1/2 c. sliced white onions or one medium onion
1/2 c. chopped cilantro
1/2 c. sliced red peppers or one pepper
1/2 c. sliced red peppers or one red pepper
4 tbsp. chopped garlic
1/2 tsp. granulated garlic
1 tbsp. paprika
1/2 tsp. red pepper flakes
4 tbsp. coconut amino
1.5 c. sliced snow peas
1/2 tsp. ground cumin
1 tsp. dried or fresh thyme
6 tbsp. olive oil

Slice the chicken breast lengthwise at 3/4 inches wide and set to the side. Wash and take out the seeds of the peppers and slice lengthwise, along with the onion. Heat 3 tablespoons of the olive oil in a large cooking pot or sauté pan and sauté the peppers, onions, and fresh garlic and set to the side. In a small cooking pot, boil water and blanch the snow peas for 2 minutes. Remove and stop the cooking process in an ice bath then remove. Allow to drain and set to the side. Remove the peppers, onions, and garlic and set to the side in a small pot. With the rest of the oil in the same pan or pot, cook the chicken on high heat for 3 to 5 minutes. Add the coconut amino and cook for an additional 2 minutes. Add the rest of the ingredients, leaving the paprika, scallions, and cilantro for the last. After you have cooked for the additional 2 minutes on medium to high heat, add the snow peas and cook for 2 minutes. Serve at once.

Paleo/Keto Bacon Chicken

3–5 portions

This special chicken and bacon are made with either coconut cream or only coconut mild, dairy-free and is the best of what paleo and keto are made of. From the very beginning, when I started to make this recipe, I was always asked to make it again. Until now, nobody has turned down this chicken recipe. Two days ago, in this time of the COVID-19 pandemic, I was over to my neighbor and made this recipe for about twenty people, and it was a winner as it usually is, so I hope whoever will be preparing it will enjoy it the way I did.

2.5 lb. chicken thighs cut into cubes
1 lb. of smoked bacon
1 tsp. ground cumin
1 tbsp. granulated garlic
1 tbsp. chopped fresh garlic
1 c. chopped white or yellow onions
1/2 c. coconut milk
1/2 c. coconut cream
2 tbsp. tomato paste
1 tsp. cayenne pepper
1 tbsp. sweet paprika
1 tsp. chopped dried or fresh thyme
1 c. chopped cilantro
1 tsp. black pepper
1 tbsp. salt

Chop the bacon and cook on medium to high heat in a large cooking pot until crispy. Remove bacon and set to the side. In the same pot, add the chicken thighs and onions and cook for 5 minutes, stirring and mixing. Add tomato paste, fresh garlic, and paprika. Cook for an additional 3 minutes on medium to high heat. Add the coconut cream and milk and cook for 3 minutes. Season with salt and pepper. Now add the bacon and cilantro. Allow simmer for 10 minutes on medium heat.

Paleo/Keto Braised Coconut Curry Chicken

4–6 portions

If the person or persons like food cooked with coconut like the way I do, you will enjoy this coconut curry chicken in a different way than you usually do because it's not only gluten-free, but it's healthy and good for you. I hope you enjoy this curry coconut. There are many different versions of curry coconut. You can use cream or milk or coconut cream or even both.

3 lb. boneless chicken things
1/2 c. cubed carrots
1/2 c. diced onions
1/2 c. cubed sweet potatoes   combine as a five-spice mix
4 tbsp. curry powder
4 tbsp. chopped fresh garlic   curry powder
1 tbsp. chopped lemongrass   cayenne pepper
1/2 tbsp. ginger   sweet paprika
1 tsp. cayenne pepper   cumin powder
1 tsp. sweet paprika   coriander powder
1 tsp. cumin powder
2 bay leaves
1/2 tsp. coriander (optional)
1 tbsp. salt and black
pepper mix
6 tbsp. olive oil
2.5 c. coconut mil
2 tbsp. arrowroot (1/2 c. water), mix together in a cup

Skin and clean the chicken thighs lengthwise and season with the five-spice mix. In a large pot, heat the olive oil and brown the chicken, onions, and garlic for 3 to 5 minutes on high. Add the cubed carrots and sweet potatoes, 2 cups of coconut milk, the ginger, and bay leaves and simmer for 10–15 minutes on low to medium heat. Now add the rest of the coconut milk and simmer for another 10 minutes on medium heat. Season with salt and pepper and then thicken with the 1/2 cup arrowroot mix. Serve hot or with warm cauliflower rice or roasted vegetables.

Paleo/ Keto Sauces or Dips

Make at home your dip or sauce!

Chimichurri Sauce and Marinade

4–6 servings

This sauce/marinade I've used as a dip and marinade is very tasty and can also be used on grilling meats.

6 cloves of chopped fresh garlic
1 tsp. red pepper flakes
3.5 c. olive oil
1/2 c. fresh chopped cilantro
6 tbsp. red vinegar
1/2 c. lemon juice
1/2 tsp. lemon zest
1 tbsp. mustard (optional)
1/2 tsp. of salt and black pepper mixture

In a blender or a food processor, add the garlic and lemon juice, blending and adding the oil and cilantro gradually. Blend the pepper flakes and the rest of the ingredients to the blender until somewhat smooth for 2 minutes. Use and dip marinade on your favorite grilled meats. When done, store away in a jar or container in the refrigerator until ready for use.

Lime Cilantro Sauce or Dip

4–6 servings

In this recipe, I'm specifying the mustard because it's paleo, and it's high in mustard flavor—something I use a lot at home.

    1 c. fresh lime juice
    1.5 c. olive oil
    1.5 c. chopped cilantro
    1/2 c. white vinegar
    1 tbsp. whole grain mustard
    1.5 tbsp. Grey Poupon Dijon mustard
    1/2 tsp. salt and pepper mixture

In a blender, combine the vinegar, mustard, and lime juice. Turn on the blender and blend by adding the olive oil a little at a time. Blend all ingredients for 2–3 minutes and season with salt and pepper. Keep refrigerated. You may use it as a dip or sauce on your favorite meat.

Dill and Honey Sauce

4–6 servings

This smooth-tasting dill recipe is as good and as fresh as you will get. You may find many blends and recipes in ways you may not understand, but the blend of fresh parsley and honey is as tasty as you will taste.

> 1 c. chopped fresh parsley
> 1 c. chopped fresh dill
> 2 c. olive oil
> 1/2 c. red wine vinegar
> 2 tbsp. mustard
> 1 tsp. of salt and pepper mixture
> 2 tbsp. honey

In a food processor or blender, add the mustard, vinegar, and honey and blend by slowly adding the olive oil until a smooth consistency. Season with salt and pepper. You may also adjust with a little more honey if needed. Transfer to a jar or plastic container and store in a cool place and use on your favorite fish or chicken.

Paleo/ Keto and Vegan Salad

Tropical Vegan Salad

2–4 portions

This interesting salad can be presented in many ways and be made in many ways. This recipe can be made with feta cheese, watermelon, and olives and can also be made with avocado.

>   3 c. cubed pineapple
>   2 c. sliced English cucumbers cut in half moon
>   1/2 c. thinly sliced red onions
>   1/2 c. chopped cilantro
>   1/2 c. sliced red peppers

Dressing
>   1/2 c. honey
>   4 tbsp. lime juice
>   1 tbsp. lime zest
>   2 tbsp. teriyaki
>   1 tbsp. chopped mint (optional)
>   1/2 tsp. salt and white pepper mixture

In a small bowl, combine and mix all ingredients and set to the side. In a large bowl, add the pineapple, cucumbers, onions, and peppers. Dress with the dressing and the chopped cilantro. Gently mix all ingredients in a bowl. Place in the refrigerator until ready to use.

Spinach Dinner Salad

4–6 portions

Take this spinach salad and enjoy it. I made this salad so many times that I can't count how many times, and to my recall, nobody has said, "No, I don't like it." It's a happy salad, tasty, beautiful in colors, and is very inviting, and it looks nice. When eating paleo and vegan, you can omit the cheese. If eating as keto, you may have some cheese.

12 oz. fresh baby spinach, cleaned and patted dry
1 c. sliced strawberries
1 c. fresh blueberries
1/2 c. chopped fresh mangoes
1/2 c. sliced avocado
1/2 c. half-sliced yellow pear cherry tomatoes
1/2 c. artisan blush tiger cherry tomatoes
1 c. cubed feta cheese (optional)
1/4 c. shredded carrots
1/4 c. shredded red cabbage

Dressing
2 tbsp. Dijon mustard
1/2 c. olive oil
1/2 tbsp. lemon zest
2 tbsp. lemon juice
4 tbsp. honey
1/4 c. pineapple juice
1/2 tsp. kosher salt and white pepper
1 tbsp. minced shallots

In a large salad bowl, combine spinach greens and all ingredients and place them in the refrigerator. In a small bowl or blender, combine mustard, lemon juice, and honey and blend for about a minute or until smooth. Add the lemon zest, pineapple juice, and oil. Slowly adjust with the salt and pepper. Mix with the salad when ready and serve.

Paleo/ Keto and Vegan Snack

Midday Snack

In the recipe, it calls for currants. Some people use raisins, but I find raisins to be too large, and if you were thinking of using sultanas, they are, in my opinion, too showy, so you can stick with currants for the original result in taste I'm looking for.

    1/2 c. pumpkin seeds
    1 c. currants
    1/2 c. sesame seeds
    1/2 c. grated coconut
    2 tbsp. vanilla extract
    1/2 c. honey
    1/2 c. maple syrup
    1/2 c. slivered almonds
    1/2 c. quick-cook oatmeal
    Preheat oven to 350° F.

Prepare a large sheet or baking pan with parchment paper and set it to the side. In a large bowl, add all ingredients one at a time and mix well. Then pour on the prepared sheet pan or pans and bake for 10–15 minutes, turning every 5 minutes in order for it not to burn.

Allow the maple syrup and honey to caramelize and set. Remove from oven and set to cool before cutting to desired sizes. Enjoy at home, looking at your favorite program on TV, take to the park, or you may share with others. Shelf life is about 5 days at room temperature.

Full-Proof Snack
Vegetable Snack

This is a healthy paleo/keto and vegan snack. You may add other vegetables to have more variety, but the way it is, it goes very well together. It is something you can take to the beach, to the park, to the movies or just after a workout at the gym.

1 lb. celery
1 green bell pepper
1 red bell pepper
1 yellow bell pepper
0.5 lb. carrots

Take a peeler and peel the celery for a smoother bite. Cut to 1.5 to 2 inches in length. Wash and cut the pepper also into 1.5 to 2 inches in length if you were able to find the size peppers you need. Wash and peel the carrots and cut them into 1.5 to 2 inches in length and set all to the side. You may also wrap the vegetable in a damp kitchen paper to keep it moist in the refrigerator.

Dip
2 avocados
1 jalapeño (seeded)
1 whole medium tomato (cubed)
2 tbsp. chopped fresh cilantro
1 tsp. salt and pepper mix
2 tbsp. chopped red onions
1/2 tsp. fresh garlic
1 tbsp. red vinegar
1 tbsp. lemon juice
2 tbsp. olive oil

In a food processor, add the avocado olive oil and cubed tomato and blend for 1 minute. Add the other ingredients and blend for another minute. The mixture should not be smooth but chunky. Place in the refrigerator until ready to use.

Index

Roasted Cauliflower with Garlic
41
Roasted Collard Greens 32
Roasted Marble Sweet Potatoes
74
roasting 25, 37, 40, 67
rutabaga 15, 22
salmon 4, 18, 42
salt 10, 18, 19, 29, 30, 32, 35,
36, 37, 38, 39, 40, 41, 44,
45, 46, 47, 48, 49, 50, 55,
56, 57, 58, 59, 60, 61, 62,
63, 64, 65, 67, 68, 69, 71,
72, 74, 78, 79, 80, 81, 85,
86, 87, 91, 92, 93, 98
salting 25
sautéing 25
scallions 48, 58, 63, 64, 65, 67,
69, 74, 75, 76, 77
seaweed 15, 22
shallots 66, 92
Shredded Brussels Sprouts with
Porcini or Champignon
Mushrooms 29
shrimps 13, 47
smoking 25
snow peas 8, 9, 18, 76
soursop 15
Southwestern Beef and Rice 70
Spaghetti Squash Lasagna 35
Spicy Chicken and Sprouts 69
spinach 5, 16, 17, 24, 67, 92, 93
Spinach Dinner Salad 92
squash 16, 22, 30, 35, 36, 42
star fruit 15

steaming 25
strawberries 4, 17, 19, 21, 24,
49, 92
Stuffed Zucchini Boats 72
sunflower seeds 4, 14, 19, 23
super snacks 21
sweet potatoes 15, 18, 22, 36,
63, 75
Sweet Potato Hash 63
Sweet Potato Salad 67
Swiss chard 4, 22
teriyaki 91
thyme 72, 76, 78
tilapia 18, 50
toasting 25
tomatoes 16, 17, 18, 44, 47, 59,
60, 61, 62, 70, 72, 73, 92
tomato paste 16, 18, 70, 72, 73,
78, 79
Tropical Vegan Salad 91
tuna 16, 18, 19
turnips 15, 22
vanilla extract 18, 97
vegan 1, 3, 7, 11, 19, 23, 24, 30,
41, 44, 57, 61, 67, 69, 74,
92, 98
vegetable broth 32
Vegetable Snack 98
venison 13, 14
walnuts 4, 23
water 3, 4, 19, 30, 36, 37, 45,
46, 49, 58, 62, 64, 65, 72,
77, 80
wild boar 14

About the Author

As a young man growing up, my parents showed and taught me to be all you can be, and at the beginning, I didn't know the meaning, but after some time, I got the whole picture.

After my first cookbook (*Hosting the Holidays*), there was so much more on my mind that it took me a few weeks to start writing another book (*My Cooking: Cookbook*).

I love writing because after so many years living in Europe, US, and Asia, I found that there is so much about food people don't know. As simple as a cup of rice may seem, it is not as simple as we may think it is because there are so many different kinds of rice and so many ways we can prepare it.

As a chef, I think a lot of considerations have to be made. We have so many people with so many issues like allergies to products and celiac disease; we have vegans, vegetarians, people with onion and celery allergies, and people who can't have dairy. I know a young lady who worked for me. She couldn't touch or smell pineapple, but again, there are so many who don't take those things or even have in mind. And lastly but not least, sugar. We have so many with diabetes. I hope there would be a government body with better control on how much sugar is used in our daily food consumption because there are so many ways companies use some fancy word for *sugar*. But if it's not sugar, there is a way to sweeten something, a chemical enhancement that is not good for our bodies. Companies use it and are only thinking about profit and not our health.

www.ingramcontent.com/pod-product-compliance
Lightning Source LLC
Chambersburg PA
CBHW031338160726
47993CB00002B/731